Thirty-Two
ELEPHANT REMINDERS

A Book of Healthy Rules

Mary M. McKee

nc.

Mary M. McKee
Minnetonka, Minnesota 55343

Library of Congress Cataloging-in-Publication Data

McKee, Mary (Mary Michele)
   Thirty-two elephant reminders.

   1. Interpersonal relations. 2. Interpersonal relations
— Problems, exercises, etc. 3. Conduct of life.
I. Title. II. Title: 32 elephant reminders.
HMI32.M3743   1987   302.3'4   87-23701
ISBN 0-932194-59-1

©   1987   Mary M. McKee

ISBN 0-932194-59-1

Published by Health Communications, Inc.
Enterprise Center
3201 S.W. 15th Street
Deerfield Beach, FL 33442

DEDICATED TO

Shaun & Myles

WITH *SPECIAL* THANKS TO

Anna & Diana

FOREWORD

My hope is that if you're feeling frustrated, confused or angry and you don't know why, you may find some insight with this book.

That frustration, confusion or anger may have its origin in the rules you were taught as a child. Dysfunctioning families can vary in their degree of unhealthiness. What may appear to be tolerable to one, may have been painful for another.

It is irrelevant what level of a dysfunctioning family system we grew up in. What is important is that individuals are coming to realize that the rules they were taught on how to live, no longer work for them in a positive way.

When we begin to reject the negative rules, we can be left with a void. Like when we learn how to rewalk, we need assistance. We have to learn to care for the child within us. To protect, guide and nurture that child.

This book was created to provide healthy guidelines for the people who are learning how to care for themselves and . . . eventually . . . for their children.

Love others as you love yourself. Because in order to care for others, we need to care for ourselves first.

1. Look at actions...

To find out what a person is really like, you sometimes have to look at their actions instead of their words.

People often say what they *think* others want to hear.

Do your actions go along with your words?

Q. Whose words/actions are confusing you?

1. _____

2. _____

3. _____

4. _____

2. Thru decisions we grow...

When we shelter another person, or even ourselves, from making decisions and being responsible, we rob them of the opportunity to grow.

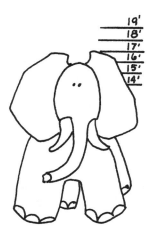

Q. What decisions are you in the process of making?

1. _____

2. _____

3. _____

4. _____

3. Love is given freely...

If you care for someone with the idea that they will return love in the same way, you could be setting yourself up for a disappointment. People are all different-they express their love in different ways. Also, people can tell the difference between love and an exchange for services.

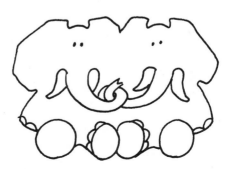

Q. How do you show your love?

1. _____

2. _____

3. _____

Q. How do other people in your life show their love for you?

1. _____

2. _____

3. _____

4. Personal rights

Sometimes, because of background, we feel we should put others before ourselves.

But think of yourself like a bank...if you don't make deposits you'll soon go broke!

You have the right and the responsibility to protect and take care of yourself.

Q. What things do you do just for yourself?

1. _____

2. _____

3. _____

4. _____

5. Self-worth...

Our sense of self-worth comes from ourselves...not from another person.

Sometimes we look to another person to make us feel worthwhile. This is placing a big burden on them and doesn't leave you with much if they go away!

Do things that make you feel good about yourself... even if no one else knows about it!

Q. What makes you feel good about yourself?

1. _____

2. _____

3. _____

4. _____

6. Have goals...

What are your goals? If you
wait for others to give them
to you, you'll miss out on the
excitement of achieving them
on your own! Plus, they may
not have the same goals!

Q. What are your goals?

1. _____

2. _____

3. _____

4. _____

7. Be an original

Why waste your time trying to be a copy when you could be an original?

We've all been given "talents" and it's up to us to use them. Don't be like the elephant who tried to be a bird. He ended up being a mediocre bird when he could have been the best of elephants!

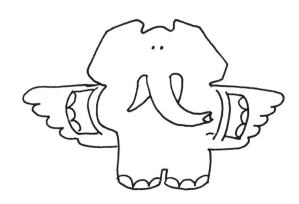

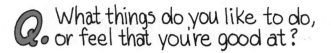

Q. What things do you like to do, or feel that you're good at?

1. _____

2. _____

3. _____

4. _____

8. Your inner voice

When we do things that aren't quite right, no one has to tell us... we know it. Sometimes we think we got away with it, or we convince ourselves that we "have to" in order to survive.

Negative actions take away our own self-respect... and we can't run away from ourselves.

Q. What are your basic beliefs and do you follow them?

1. _____

2. _____

3. _____

4. _____

9. Patterns...

Change is never comfortable. But if you seem to keep finding yourself in the same negative relationships, you might want to stop and look to see if there is a pattern. Do you want it to continue?

Q. What are some negative patterns you would like to change?

1. _____

2. _____

3. _____

4. _____

10. Changes...

To know the "right" answers is great - but for change to occur, you have to act on your knowledge.

Change is never comfortable... to you nor to others.

Q. What changes do you want to occur?

1. _____

2. _____

3. _____

Q. What actions do you need to take?

1. _____

2. _____

3. _____

11. Martyrs are uncomfortable to be around...

People who do kind acts just so others will think they're great are setting themselves up for resentment. Martyrs can become angry if the gratitude isn't enough, plus other people don't like to feel they "owe" another person.

Q. What things make you feel resentful?

1. _____

2. _____

3. _____

Q. What would happen if you stopped doing those things?

1. _____

2. _____

3. _____

12. Emotions are o. k.

We all have a right to our feelings. We can learn to express them in a positive way – and allow others to express theirs.

If we shut out our emotions, we shut the best part of us!

Q. What feelings don't you share with others?

1. _____

2. _____

3. _____

4. _____

Q. What do you think would happen if you did?

1. _____

2. _____

3. _____

4. _____

13. Big & little...

Often adults look to children for love, self-esteem and their self-worth.

Children need protection and guidance. These are basic needs and ones that will be sought after, if not met in childhood.

Q. What are some of your child's interests or abilites that they could use your help with?

1. _____

2. _____

3. _____

4. _____

14. Letting go...

Sometimes we have to let go of a relationship. We can explain that we love them, but not their behavior.

This is not abandoning them but letting them be aware of how their behavior is affecting you and themselves.

They have to make the decision of whether or not they want to change.

Q. Is there someone in your life you have to "let go" of?

1. _____

2. _____

3. _____

Q. What is the difference between helping and enabling?

1. _____

2. _____

3. _____

4. _____

15. Asking for help...

If your car doesn't work, you would not hesitate to bring it in for repair...yet many people will wait until they're broken down emotionally before they'll ask for help.

Asking for help does not show weakness—it's smart!

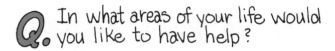

Q. In what areas of your life would you like to have help?

1. _____

2. _____

3. _____

4. _____

16. Controlling others...

You cannot control nor be responsible for another person's actions.

You are responsible for your own actions and reactions.

Q. Whose actions do you try to control or feel responsible for?

1. _____

2. _____

3. _____

4. _____

17. Buffers...

Sometimes we turn to negative behavior to block out our anger...and what we're really afraid of.

NEGATIVE BEHAVIOR ➡ ANGER ➡ FEAR

Q. What buffers do you use to cover up your feelings?

1. _____

2. _____

3. _____

4. _____

18. Judging others...

People with the wisdom and knowledge to judge others... rarely do.

This applies to ourselves. Don't judge yourself too harshly... remember the positive progress you have made.

Q. What are some things you are having difficulty forgiving yourself for?

1. _____

2. _____

3. _____

4. _____

19. No 1st-time experts...

Teenage years are meant for finding out about themselves, adjusting to a world outside the home

We wouldn't expect anyone, at any age, to be an expert at something totally new to them.

Q. What things did you experience as a teenager that you had difficulty in handling?

1._____

2._____

3._____

4._____

20. Express yourself...

It is difficult being with someone who expects you to read their mind.

Besides building up resentment on both sides - the other person might pick up the wrong message!

Q. What likes/dislikes would you like to express?

1. _____

2. _____

3. _____

Q. What do you think would happen if you did express them?

1. _____

2. _____

3. _____

21. Save yourself...

Often we think that if we're weak or act helpless, others will come to our rescue or will love us more.

But we shouldn't confuse love with pity...or underestimate the importance of recognizing our strengths.

Q. When you were little, what did you want to be when you grew up?

1. _____

2. _____

3. _____

Q. What are some things you do well today?

1. _____

2. _____

3. _____

22. Anger is a message...

Anger can tell us something is not right, or that we need to protect ourselves or others.

Anger does not mean hate. Anger is an emotion. You don't have a choice about being angry, you just are and it's o.k. We can learn how to use anger as a useful tool to understanding ourselves.

Q. How was anger expressed in your family when you were a child?

1. _____

2. _____

3. _____

Q. How do you express your anger today?

1. _____

2. _____

3. _____

23. Controlling with "niceness..."

People can use their sensitivity or "niceness" to get others to protect or to get angry for them.

This can be just as controlling just as much as a loud, domineering person.

"Nice" people are difficult to relate to in an honest give-and-take relationship.

Q. What things do you talk about wanting to change, but haven't done anything about?

1. _____

2. _____

3. _____

Q. What would happen if you began to deal with them?

1. _____

2. _____

3. _____

24. Healthy love

A healthy relationship is when you come away feeling better about yourself.

A healthy relationship does not make you feel shameful or frightened of being judged.

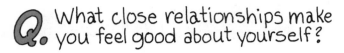 What close relationships make you feel good about yourself?

1._____

2._____

3._____

4._____

25. Others can be our mirrors...

We sometimes can experience a strong reaction towards another person—it could be a reflection of an unresolved problem of our own.

Or it can be something we like about ourselves.

Q. What type of people upset you?

1. _____

2. _____

3. _____

Q. What type of people are you attracted to ?

1. _____

2. _____

3. _____

26. Healthy boundaries...

We all have a right to set our own personal boundaries.

These boundaries can apply to our bodies, possessions or what others say or do to us.

It is important that children know this at an early age.

Q. What healthy boundaries do you want to set up for yourself?

1. _____

2. _____

3. _____

4. _____

27. Share, don't dump . . .

We cannot put the responsibility on others to "fix" situations for us.

We can share our thoughts to get healthy feedback, or alternatives, in order for us to take care of the situations.

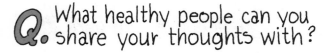

Q. What healthy people can you share your thoughts with?

1. _____

2. _____

3. _____

4. _____

28. Special others...

Do you find yourself treating strangers nicer than you do those you love?

Those closest to us need kindness & courtesy too.

When we don't treat them well, it sends out a confusing message.

Q. What people mean the most to you?

1. _____

2. _____

3. _____

4. _____

29. Over-using our heads...

The longest 18 inches can be from our head to our heart.

We often are "shamed" out of our feelings. Emotions don't have an I.Q., but they are important to our well being.

Your feelings are not stupid!

Q. How do you feel when you are telling someone how you feel?

1. _____

2. _____

Q. When you were a child, who would you talk to about your feelings?

1. _____

2. _____

Q. After you told them how you felt, how would they respond?

1. _____

2. _____

30. Live your own life ...

We can waste a lot of time and energy if we live for the "theys" of the world.

"They" wouldn't approve ...

"They" made me do it ...

Do you run your life on the "theys" of the world instead of doing what you think is right?

Q. Who are the "theys" in your life?

1. _____

2. _____

3. _____

Q. Who are some people you respect or admire?

1. _____

2. _____

3. _____

Positive Reminders

☑ 1. LOOK AT A PERSON'S ACTIONS

☑ 2. THRU DECISIONS WE GROW

☑ 3. LOVE IS GIVEN FREELY

☑ 4. WE EACH HAVE RIGHTS

☑ 5. SELF-WORTH COMES FROM WITHIN

☑ 6. GO AFTER YOUR GOALS

☑ 7. BE YOURSELF

☑ 8. MAKE YOURSELF PROUD

☑ 9. LOOK AT NEGATIVE PATTERNS

☑ 10. ACT ON YOUR KNOWLEDGE

☑ 11. MARTYRS ARE UNCOMFORTABLE
        TO BE AROUND

☑ 12. EMOTIONS ARE O.K.

☑ 13. CHILDREN NEED GUIDANCE & PROTECTION

☑ 14. LETTING GO

☑ 15. TAKE CARE OF YOURSELF

- ☑ 16. YOU CAN'T CONTROL OTHERS
- ☑ 17. LOOK AT YOUR FEARS
- ☑ 18. DON'T JUDGE YOURSELF OR OTHERS
- ☑ 19. BE PATIENT WITH TEENAGERS
- ☑ 20. EXPRESS YOURSELF
- ☑ 21. ACTING HELPLESS ISN'T HEALTHY
- ☑ 22. ANGER CAN TELL YOU SOMETHING
- ☑ 23. BEWARE OF ACTING FOR OTHERS
- ☑ 24. HEALTHY LOVE FEELS NICE
- ☑ 25. OTHERS CAN BE YOUR REFLECTION
- ☑ 26. DEVELOPE HEALTHY BOUNDARIES
- ☑ 27. SHARE ... DON'T DUMP
- ☑ 28. SHOW YOUR LOVE
- ☑ 29. HEAD & HEART = BALANCE
- ☑ 30. LIVE YOUR OWN LIFE
- ☑ 31. BALANCE CAN FEEL DIFFERENT
- ☑ 32. BE PATIENT WITH YOURSELF

32. Be patient with yourself...

Beating yourself up about not being well right away can keep you unhealthy.

Be patient with yourself! When you are used to doing things one way for a long time, you can't expect to correct it overnight!

No one is perfect.

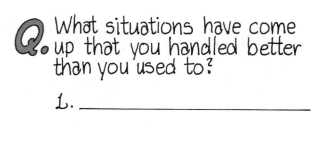

Q. What situations have come up that you handled better than you used to?

1. _____

_____

2. _____

_____

3. _____

_____

31. Balance your life...

When we begin to find balance in our lives, it can be rather uncomfortable at first.

We've been used to extreme highs & lows and can miss the excitement of these extremes.

Living in pain was almost more comfortable because it was all we'd known.

Having a balanced life can feel boring at first.

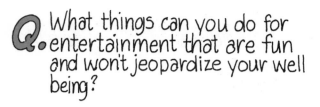

Q. What things can you do for entertainment that are fun and won't jeopardize your well being?

1. _____

2. _____

3. _____

4. _____

NOTES

NOTES

NOTES

NOTES

Mary McKee was born and raised in Northern Minnesota where she has a studio named Strom Stuga, which means "river cabin" in Swedish. She obtained her fine arts degree, then worked in the graphic arts field where her work has won awards in commercial illustration and design.

In recent years, Mary has devoted her artistic energies to portraying life issues around her. She concentrates on several medias, often combining her writings with pencil, gouache and oil paintings, which allow her to express her ideas in a unique style.

She is married and is the mother of two grown sons.